Musical Projects and Games
by Nigel Osborne

Although for convenience and logical development, this book is grouped in sections under the headings Sound, Rhythm, Pitch and Form, it is not necessary to work all the way through each section before moving to the next. A more varied approach will be achieved by working the first or second exercise from one section and then similarly with the next, and so on. Whichever approach is used, a discussion of the material of each page, will help the start of the creative process, although where imaginative solutions are called for, you must be careful not to enforce your creative ideas.

The material in this book encourages both a carefully structured approach to creative work (as for instance in so much jazz) and a free imaginative approach. For the fullest development, both are necessary. The structured way, by itself, can lead to the reproduction of expressionless ideas, the free, to disorganised sound, unrelated to music. As with most things in life, a balanced diet produces the healthiest results.

Many of the exercises, games and projects lend themselves to further development and this is particularly so with the pitch section, where, after working with the strictly limited pentatonic range of sounds, the pupils may wish to explore further the expressive potential of other scales, both traditional and new.

Your plan of use may at times be influenced by group size. As will be seen from the list, some pages imply group work, some class work and others, individual activity. All units are critical in the development of creative work; the class, lead by you, the group, interacting between its members and of course the individual expressing his own ideas in the medium.

First Published 1975
This Edition © 1989

Prelude

An imprint of the
Education Division of
International Music Publications

Exclusive Distributors
International Music Publications
Southend Road, Woodford Green,
Essex IG8 8HN, England.

Photocopying of this copyright material is illegal
and may lead to prosecution.

1-2-50620

Reference List

Page	Group	Class	Individual
3			★
4			★
5	★	★	
6	★		
7	★		
8			★
9			★
10–11		★	
12–13	★	★	
14	★		
15	★		
16		★	★
17		★	★
18	★		
19			★
20–21		★	
22	★		
23	★	★	
24	★		
25	★		
26	★	★	★
27			★
28–29	★	★	
30	★		
31			★
32			★

SOUND
DISCOVERY

1. SOUNDS AND PLACES

Make a list of the sounds you would be likely to hear in each of the following places:

    a street
    a market
    a railway station
    an airport
    a forest
    a farmyard
    by the sea

Some you will be able to check. For others you will have to use your memory or imagination.

2. THINKING ABOUT SOUND

There are many ways of describing sound. We say a sound is

>loud or soft
>high or low
>long or short
>near or far
>beautiful or ugly

and so on.

For the moment let us look at loud or soft and high or low. Copy the table below and enter in the centre column the list of sounds you have collected. Then in the other columns tick whether you think the sound is loud or soft, high or low.

The letter *f* means loud.

The letter *p* means soft.

f	*p*	SOUND	high	low
✓		e.g. traffic		✓
	✓	seagull	✓	

Try and list some more examples.

3. WHAT DO SOUNDS MEAN?

Some sounds have little meaning. Others, like speech, are the ways we understand one another. Car horns and bicycle bells are also sounds which carry important messages. How many more examples can you think of?

Even sounds which are not meant to be messages may sometimes tell us something. At the sound of an approaching car, we take care. The breaking of a twig in a forest might tell us an animal is near.

GAMES
FLOTILLA

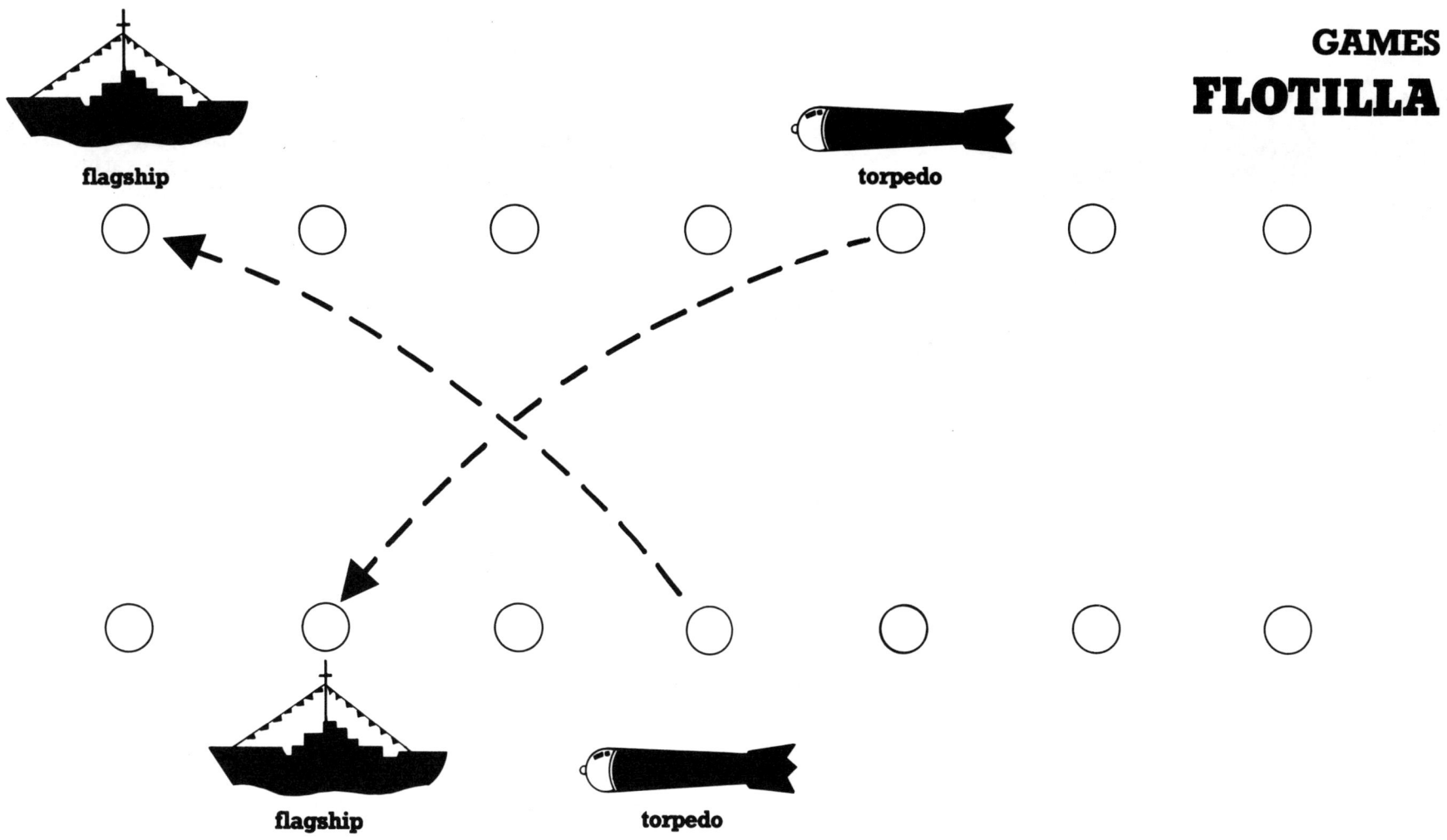

1. Form two equal teams. Each team chooses one person to be a **flagship**, and one person to be a **torpedo**. Keep your choice a secret from the enemy!
2. Take a percussion instrument each, and form two battle lines facing each other a fair distance apart.
3. Blindfold the **torpedoes**.
4. The **flagships** now show where they are. Each team guides its torpedo towards the enemy's flagship by sound alone; louder sounds to the left guide the torpedo leftwards; louder sounds to the right, rightwards.
5. The first team to knock out the enemy's flagship is the winner.

Invent games of your own using the same idea — soccer, golf or bowling perhaps.

COMPOSITION

1. POEMS

Work in groups. Choose one person to read. Everyone else must work out descriptive sounds to go with the words. Use voices or instruments. Choose your instruments carefully and be sure to explore them fully.

TRADITIONAL (MARSHALL ISLANDS)

STORM TIDE ON MEJIT

The wind's spine is broken,
It blows less,
We perform the wind-tabu,
It grows still, still,
Wholly still,
The calm, the calm,
The wind-tabu, e,
Makes calm, calm, calm.
The surf, surf, surf,
The surf, surf, surf,
The surf, surf, surf,
Plunges, roars,
Plunges, roars,
Plunges, roars,
It flows up.
The sea covers the beach with foam,
It is full of the finest sand,
Stirring up the ground, stirring up the ground.
It slaps, slaps, slaps,
Slaps, slaps, slaps
On the beach, and roars.

Write your own poem about the wind, the sea or the weather and work out sounds to fit with it.

2. FILM MUSIC

Try and imagine some scenes from films you may have seen or heard about. The illustrations below will give you some ideas.

Work in groups and make up sounds to fit each of the scenes. Use percussion instruments. Aim to make as much contrast as possible between scenes.

Now collect your own ideas for a film. Use cuttings from magazines, colour slides or your own drawings. Make up a score to fit your film.

RHYTHM

DISCOVERY

1. RHYTHMS AROUND US

There are many rhythmic sounds in the world about us:

>   clocks
>   trains
>   footsteps

and even sometimes words.
   How many examples can you think of? Make a list.

2. OUR OWN RHYTHMS

Most of the actions we perform with our bodies are rhythmic, like:

>   breathing
>   running
>   hammering
>   sawing.

   Make a list of as many examples as you can think of.

3. RHYTHMS WE DO NOT HEAR

There are rhythms in the world which we do not hear. We feel them or see them, like a human pulse or the flashing of a lighthouse. Even the rising and setting of the sun forms a sort of rhythm, although it is very slow indeed.
   Write down any more examples of this kind you can think of.

4. THINKING ABOUT RHYTHM

How do we describe a rhythm? The simplest way is by the speed of its pulse. Some rhythms are fast, some slow. Deep in our mind, we compare them with out heartbeat. Actions or music which are faster than our heartbeat seem exciting, slower than our heartbeat, relaxing.

We can also describe rhythms as even or uneven. Walking and running are fairly even. But the ticking of a clock is often uneven. Most clocks have long and short ticks in the pattern.

Copy the table below and enter the rhythms you have collected in the centre column. Mark the columns which best describe your rhythm.

Some rhythms, like trains, may be fast or slow, so mark both columns.

5. WHAT IS RHYTHM USED FOR?

Rhythm is part of the natural world around us. It is used by man in his everyday life. It can help people move in time together. This is important when they want to do a job together, or march in step.

Work songs and march tunes have strong rhythms which help people to work steadily and move along in time.

Rhythm may also be used to send messages, like morse code at sea. In the dark forests of Africa, people signal to each other with drum beats. The sound carries from one village to the next and is called drum talk.

Can you think of any more examples of the uses of rhythm?

FAST	SLOW	RHYTHM	EVEN	UNEVEN
✓		RUNNING	✓	
	✓	WALKING	✓	
✓	✓	TRAIN		✓

FLIGHT PLAN

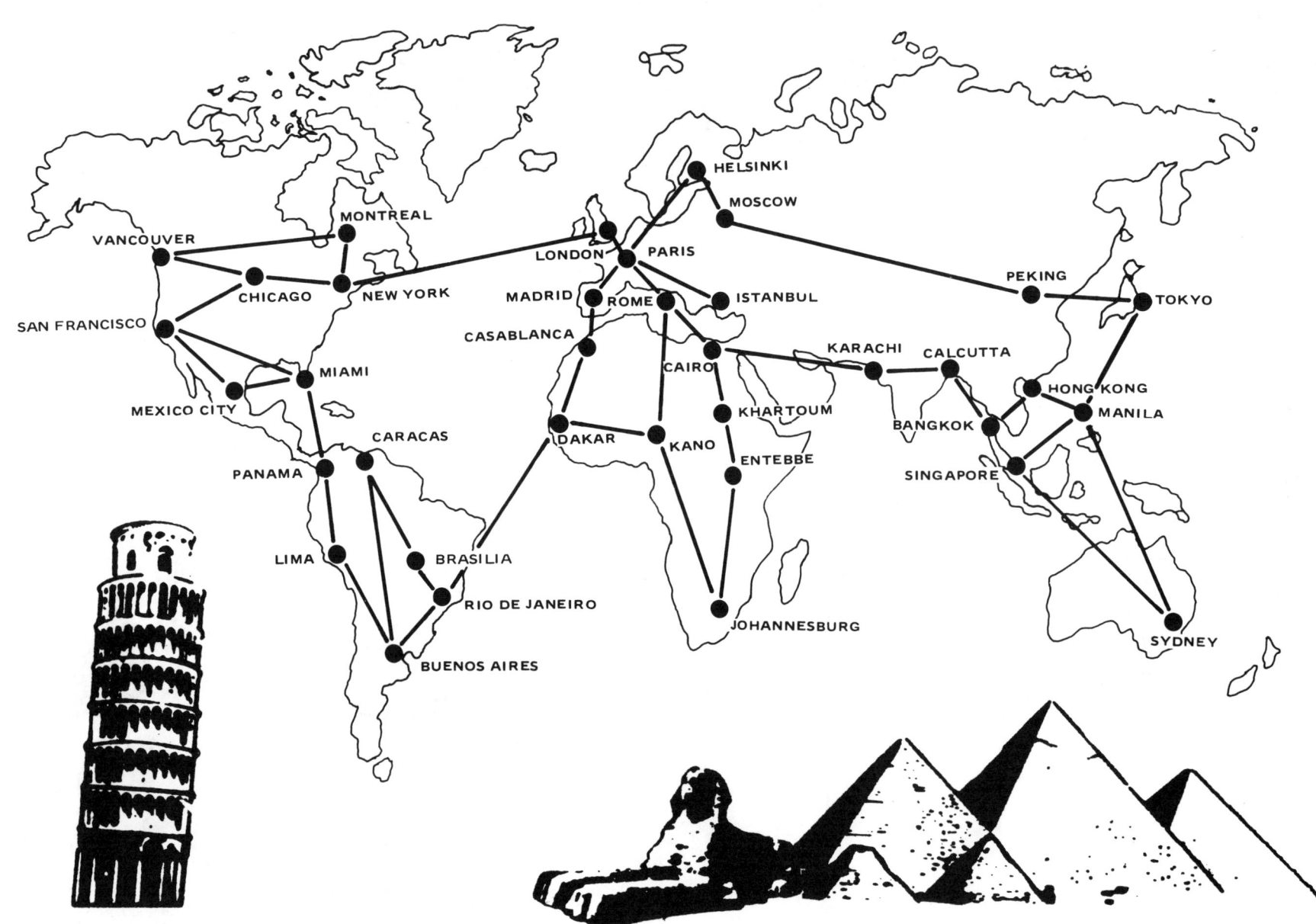

GAMES

1. Make sure that you know how to say all the names on the map.

2. Practise clapping the rhythms of the words.

   for example,

   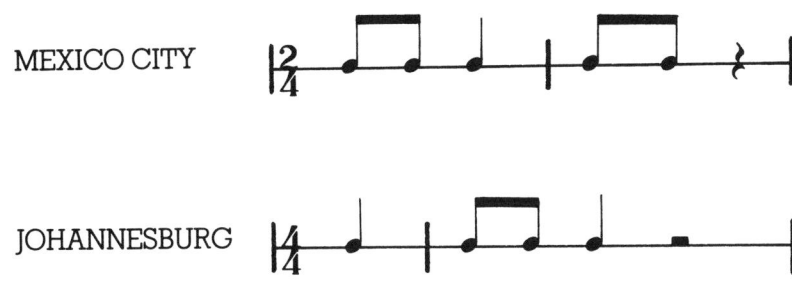

   MEXICO CITY

   JOHANNESBURG

   Notice the difference between LONDON and NEW YORK. Both have two beats, but we **lean** on the first beat of **LON**DON and the second beat of NEW **YORK**.
   This is very important.

3. The starting point of the game is LONDON. One person begins. He may 'fly' to any airport which is **one** stage away and show which he has chosen by clapping its rhythm,

   e.g.

   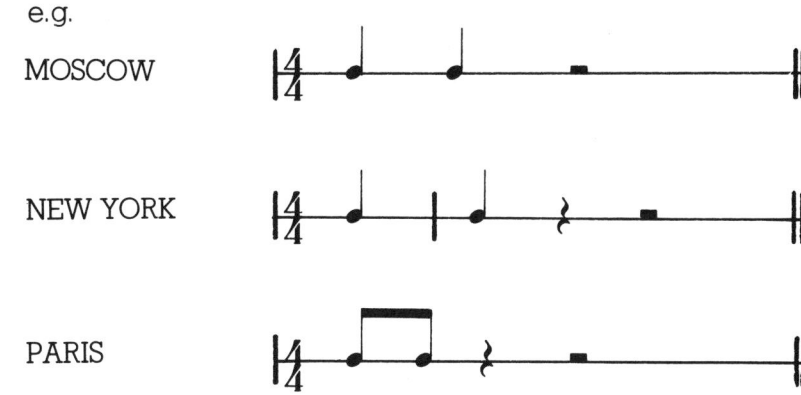

   MOSCOW

   NEW YORK

   PARIS

4. His neighbour must guess where he has landed. Then he must choose the next airport (one stage away) and clap its rhythm.

5. Try to move around the whole class in this way, piloting the plane by rhythm alone. It is interesting to see which airports of the world you visit on the way.

IMPROVISATION

1. ECHOES

Repeat these rhythmic patterns after the teacher. Clap, or use any percussion instrument.

2. IN TWO'S

Work in pairs.

One of you play the patterns, the other repeat them without looking at the music. Then change over and work through them again.

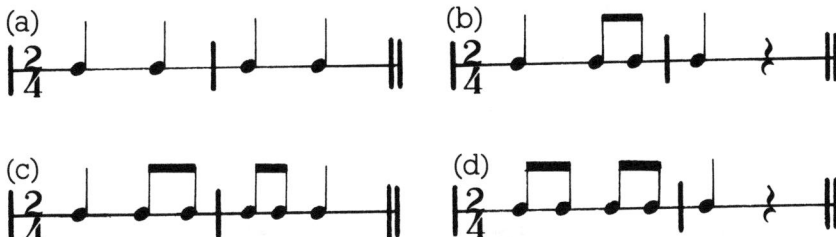

Now take turns to make up your own patterns. Play them to your partner and see if he can echo them. Try to make them the same length as the patterns in the exercise.

Take your time and think carefully.

3. QUESTIONS AND ANSWERS

Work in pairs.

One of you play the rhythms below. The other make up a reply.

It should be the same length as the question but a different pattern, like this:

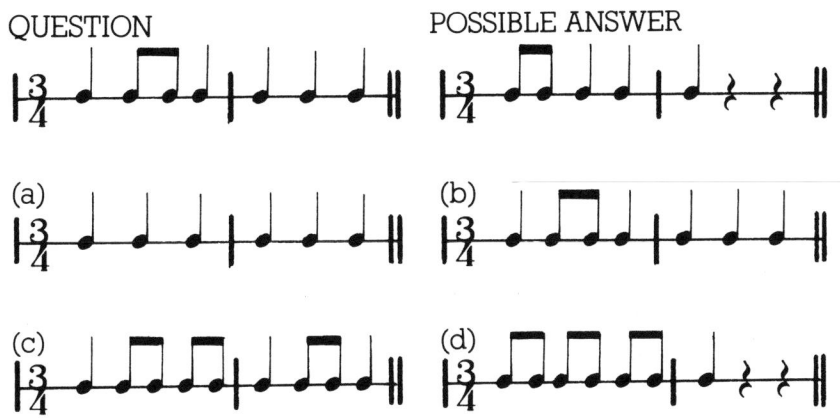

Now change places and work through them again.

4. CONVERSATIONS

Work in pairs.

You should now be ready to make up your own questions and your own replies. The secret is to keep everything as simple as possible. Try to keep to patterns with two bars of $\frac{2}{4}$ as in exercise 2. Play the exercise over to refresh your memory.

Take turns to play the questions.

5. SNAKES

Form lines of 3.

The first in line plays one of the patterns below. The second in line repeats it and adds a pattern of his own. If the third is able to repeat what the second has played and add a pattern, he moves to the front of the line and the game begins again.

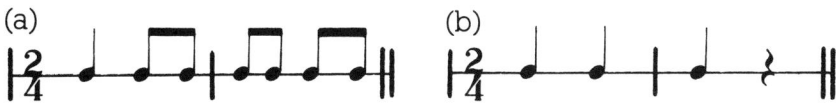

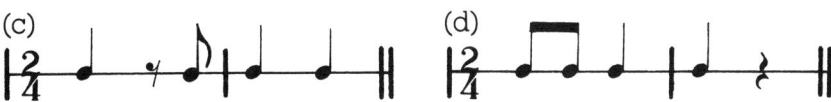

6. OSTINATO PATTERNS

These are patterns of notes which repeat themselves over and over again.

    Work in pairs. One of you play the ostinato and the other make up (improvise) a part to fit with it. Work through the following exercise taking turns to play the ostinato.

JUNGLE BEAT

for the ostinato, use a drum
for the improvisation, maracas.

MARCH

for the ostinato, use a woodblock
for the improvisation, a drum.

DANCE

for the ostinato, use a triangle
for the improvisation, a tambourine.

7. WORK RHYTHMS

Work in small groups.

Make up rhythms to fit with the activities listed. Some of you mime the activity. The rest clap or use percussion instruments. Play your ideas in time with the movement.

Can you think of any more activities which have interesting rhythms?

heaving a rope
rowing a boat
riding a bicycle
sawing wood
rocking a baby to sleep

8. CASEY JONES

Work in groups. Practise reciting the poem together and bringing out its strong rhythm.

Now choose one person to read the poem and the rest make up ostinato rhythms to fit with it.

Think of the rhythms and sounds of a train. Do not be afraid to use your voices. One person should play a regular beat to keep the rest together.

Come all you rounders, listen here,
I'll tell you the story of a brave engineer,
Casey Jones was the hogger's name,
On a six-eight-wheeler, boys, he won his fame.
Caller called Casey at half-past four,
He kissed his wife at the station door,
Mounted to the cabin with orders in his hand,
And took his farewell trip to the promised land.

Casey Jones mounted to the cabin,
Casey Jones, with his orders in his hand!
Casey Jones mounted to the cabin,
Took his farewell trip into the promised land.

'Put in your water and shovel in your coal,
Put your head out the window, watch the drivers roll,
I'll run her till she leaves the rail,
'Cause we're eight hours late with the Western Mail!'
He looked at his watch and his watch was slow,
Looked at the water and the water was low,
Turned to his fireboy and then he said
'We're bound to reach 'Frisco, but we'll all be dead!'

Casey Jones, etc.

COMPOSITION

1. HILL 'N GULLY

Here is a well-known work song. Learn to sing it as a class, to LA

* Here recorders and guitars may join in.

Now work on your own and write a part for percussion to fit with the song. It may be a one-bar pattern repeated as an ostinato. Look at the tune for ideas. Play what you have written.

2. TRYROLEAN DANCE

Copy the following and write a part for triangle over the cymbal ostinato.

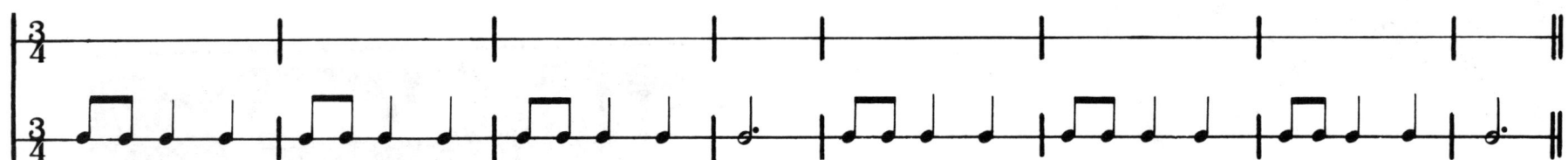

If you have difficulty, here is an idea to begin with

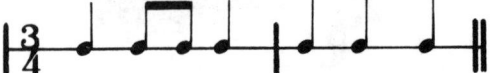

Make sure you have the right number of beats in every bar. Perform the piece to the class.

3. CALYPSO

Clap the rhythm of the ostinato together as a class.

Now copy out both lines, and write a part for woodblock. Here is a possible start:

4. THE FISHER'S LIFE

Practise reciting the poem together as a class.

Now work on your own and make up three or four ostinato patterns to fit with the rhythm of the words. Use $\frac{4}{4}$ time and try to keep the patterns one bar long.

Write them down like this:

which means that the pattern is repeated.

Choose an instrument to play each of your patterns and perform your setting to the class.

What joys attend the Fisher's Life!
Blow, winds, blow!
The fisher and his faithful wife!
Row, boys, row!
He drives no plough on stubborn land,
His fields are ready to his hand;
No nipping frosts his orchards fear,
He has his autumn all the year!

The husbandman has rent to pay,
Blow, winds, blow!
And seed to purchase every day
Row, boys, row!
But he who farms the rolling deeps,
Though never sowing, always reaps;
The ocean's fields are fair and free,
There are no rent days on the sea!

PROJECT

THE STORY OF NOAH

Now let us try and tell the story of Noah without words, using sounds alone.

Divide into three groups.

Group 1. should describe the building of the ark. Think of the various work rhythms we have discussed. Choose instruments which remind you of the tasks involved in building a ship — sawing, banging, scraping and so on. Make up ostinato rhythms for each of the activities. You may begin by playing one and add the rest in turn, building up the sound of a busy workshop.

Group 2. should describe the entry of the animals to the Ark. You will have to use a great deal of imagination to find sounds for each of the animals.

Group 3. should describe the flood and the storm. Remember that a storm usually begins quietly with raindrops, rises to a climax with thunder and lightning, and dies down gradually at the end. Do not forget the flight of the raven and the dove.

Can you think of any more stories to tell in sound?

PITCH

DISCOVERY

1. We are used to hearing melody through television, radio, records or in the concert hall.
    But there are other examples, like bird song or church bells, in the world about us.

    How many more can you think of?

2. How do we describe a melody? Here is a simple way

    The line shows the rise and fall of the song of a blackbird.
    Try to draw your answers to question 1 in the same way.

3. What are these melodies for? Most are meant to tell us something. Try to think of the reason behind each of your examples.

BURIED TREASURE

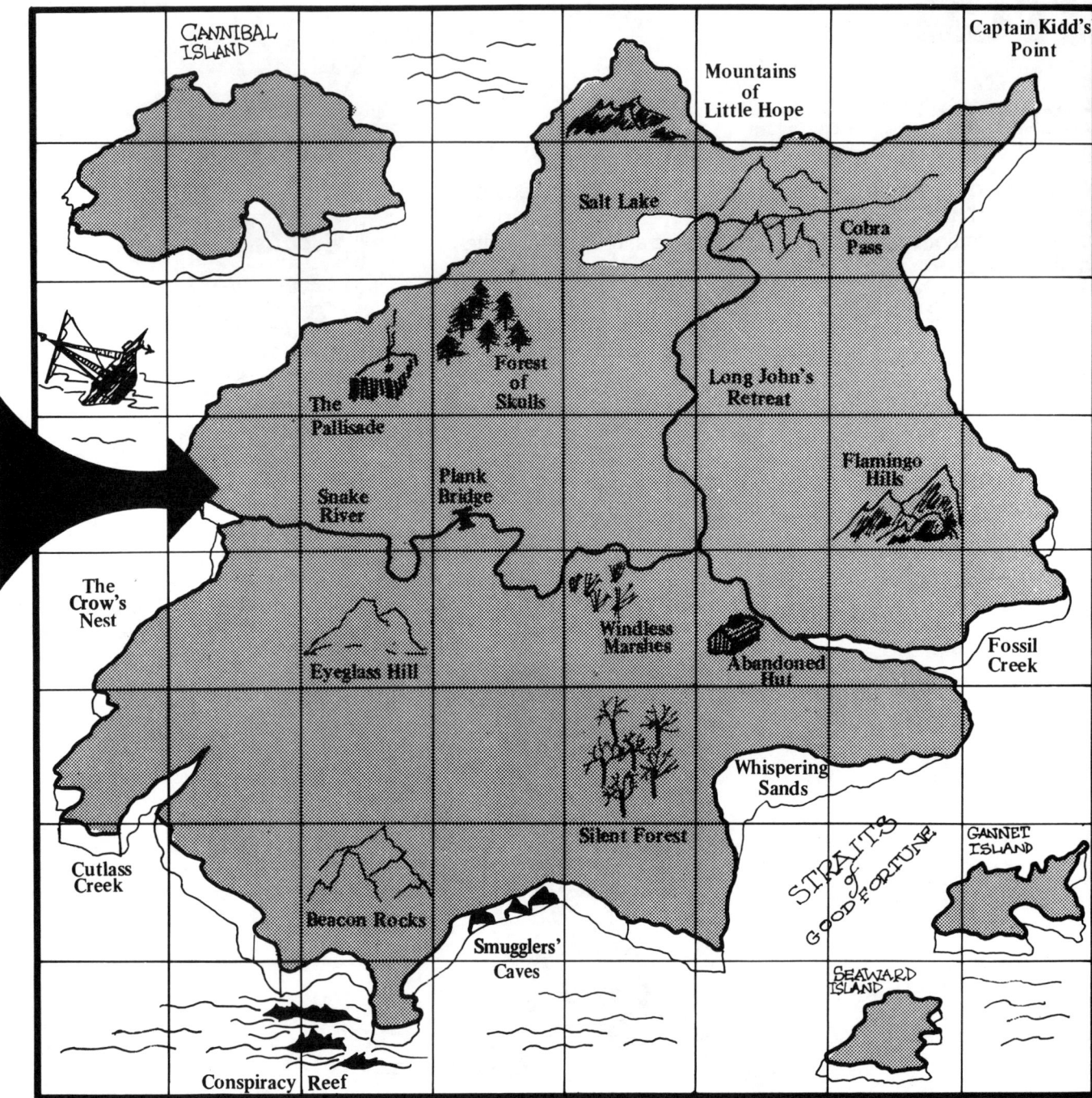

GAMES

BURIED TREASURE

1. The four patterns of notes are a secret code for giving directions — North, South, East and West.

    Play them over until you are used to them.

2. The teacher will play directions to lead you to the buried treasure. This is how to understand the code: every time the East pattern in played, move one square to the East; every time the West pattern is played, move one square to the West, and the same for North and South.

    So if the following pattern were played.

you would move four squares East from the Start, and then one square South, bringing you to the abandoned hut.

3. Form groups and take turns to give directions using recorders or glockenspiels.

4. Draw your own Treasure Island map and make up your own musical code for directions.

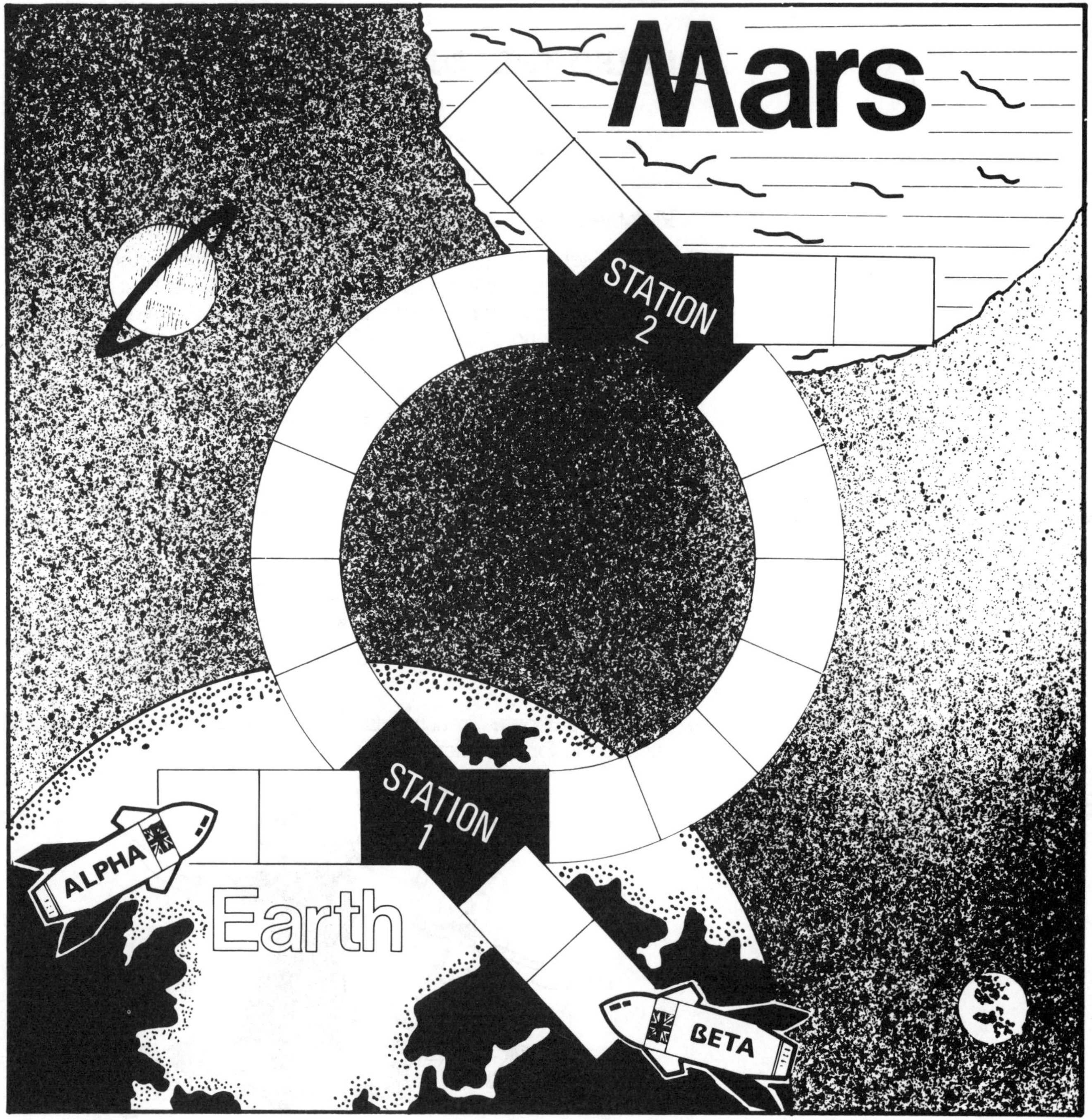

SPACE RACE

Work in two's, sharing books. Choose a rocket each, and put your counters on Go.

The teacher throws a dice. If it shows, for example 2, the teacher plays D and E. Hearing this, rocket Alpha moves 2 spaces forwards. If the dice shows, for example 6, the teacher plays DEGABD, and Alpha moves 6 spaces forwards, and so on.

The next throw of the dice is for rocket Beta, and then on, in turn.

If your partner's rocket is on a space station, your own rocket may not enter it or cross it. You must return to the previous station, or back to Go.

The first rocket to Mars is the winner.

IMPROVISATION

1. ECHOES

Repeat each of these pitch patterns after the teacher. First use your voices to 'la' or **sol-fa**. Then repeat the exercise using pitched instruments.

When you have worked through the exercise several times, try to do it without the music. Take a line at a time. Do not move on until you can repeat the patterns exactly.

2. IN TWO'S

Work in pairs.

One of you play the following patterns. The other repeat them without looking at the music. Then change places.

Now take turns to make up your own patterns. Your partner should repeat them.

Use notes G, A and B.

See Workbook 1 pages 10, 11, 15 and 16

3. QUESTIONS AND ANSWERS

Work in pairs.

One of you play the patterns below. The other make up a reply. It should be the same length as the question, but a different pattern, like this:

question

possible
answer

use G, A and B
in your replies

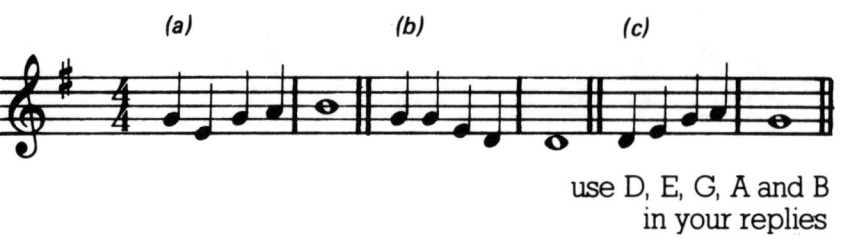

use D, E, G, A and B
in your replies

Now change places and work through them again.

4. CONVERSATIONS

Work in pairs.

You should now be ready to make up your own melodic questions and replies. Try to keep to patterns with two bars of   as in exercise 2. Play the exercise over to refresh your memories.

Take turns to play the questions. Use notes D, E, G, A and B.

5. SNAKES

Form lines of 5 or 6.

The first in line plays a note. The second in line repeats it and adds one of his own, and so on.

If the last in line is able to repeat all that has gone before, and add a note, he moves to the front of the line and the game begins again.

Use notes D, E, G, A and B.

6. APACHE WAR DANCE

Work in small groups.

One person should play the following ostinato pattern on piano or xylophone.

Take turns to make up a tune for recorder over the ostinato. Do not be afraid to make it up as you go along. Use notes D, E, G, A and B.

If you have difficulty, here is an idea to begin with

Other members of the group may

a) join in with the rhythm of the ostinato on a drum,
b) make up their own rhythms to fit in using other percussion instruments,
c) hum long notes on E (the same note as the ostinato).

Now try using voice instead of recorder.

7. THE BAGPIPES

Work in pairs.

One of you play the following ostinato on a recorder or other suitable instrument.

(a repeated long note is called a drone)

The other make up a tune for recorder to fit with it. Use notes D, E, G, A and B.

Here is a possible opening:

Now change places.

8. Work in pairs and make up your own ostinato patterns and tunes.

COMPOSITION

Here is a poem to set to music.

Hey-ho for Hallowe'en!
All the witches to be seen,
Some black, and some green,
Hey-ho for Hallowe'en!

Read the poem aloud, and you will see that the words themselves suggest a rhythm:

WITCHES' SONG

use a recorder or other pitched instrument to help you make up a tune for this rhythm.
   Try to keep to notes G, A and B only.

Write down the finished melody on manuscript paper and teach the song to the rest of the class.

COWBOY'S TUNE

Copy out and finish this tune for guitar and recorders. Use notes D, E, G, A and B.

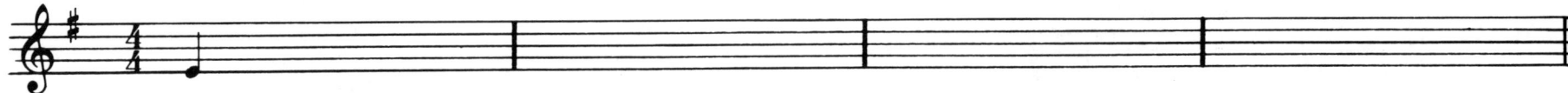

Make up an ostinato for woodblock or coconut shells to fit with it.

4. Riddles

Here are two more poems to set to music.

Use any of these notes in your melody.
To help you, the rhythms of the poems are written below.

a)

White sheep, white sheep, on a blue hill
When the wind stops, you all stand still.
When the wind blows, you run away slow,
White sheep, white sheep, where do you go?

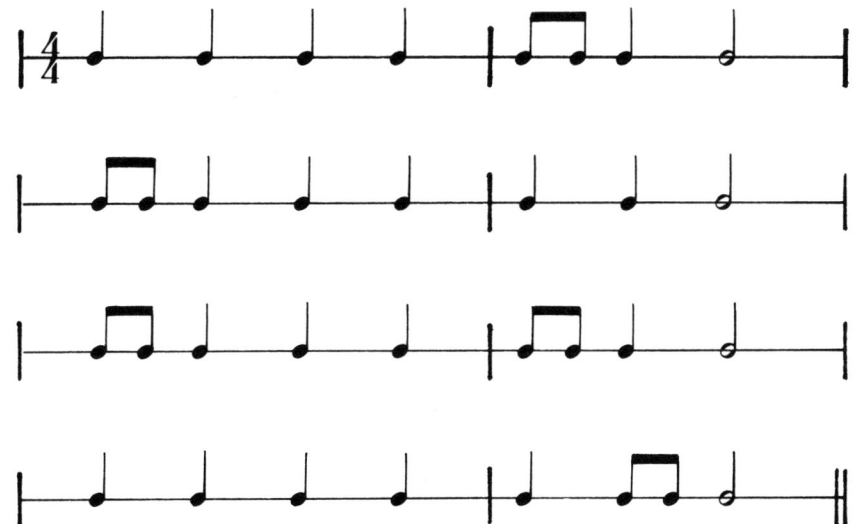

b)

Red and blue and delicate green,
The King can't catch it and neither can the Queen.
Pull it in the room and you can catch it soon.
Answer this riddle by tomorrow at noon.

answers to riddles:
a) clouds
b) rainbow

PROJECTS

SEA GIRL AND THE LAKE

a story from present-day China.

In a year of fierce drought, Chiao and his daughter Sea Girl set out from their village in the valley to cut bamboo in the nearby mountains. While they are at work, Sea Girl wanders some distance away from her father and discovers a mysterious shining lake. The water is pure and still. Nothing disturbs its surface. Even as leaves fall, a wild goose flies down and catches them in his bill.

Later, Sea Girl returns alone to the mountains to find some way of bringing the water to the village. She finds the lake again and tries to cut a channel, but the water will not flow. Tired and discouraged, she lies down under a tree. While she rests the wild goose arrives and tells her that she will not make the water flow unless she finds the golden key to the lake. With this he flies away leaving Sea Girl to search for further clues.

As she sets out she meets two parrots who tell her that the golden key is kept by the Dragon King in his magical palace. Further on she meets a peacock, who suggests that her best chance of finding the key is to draw the attention of the Dragon King's daughter. She is unable to resist the beauty of song and will surely appear if Sea Girl sings aloud some of the songs of the valley.

So Sea Girl begins her song. Very soon the Dragon King's daughter appears. Enchanted by the singing, she agrees to tell the story of the golden key. It is jealously guarded by the Dragon King and watched over by an eagle in the inner courts of the palace. During the day, the eagle holds the key in his sharp, cruel gaze. At night he folds his wings and sleeps on it in his nest.

Sea Girl and the Dragon King's daughter set out for the palace and on the way they make up a plan. When they arrive it is evening, and the eagle is asleep on the golden key. But the two girls begin to sing and the eagle is so surprised by the sound that he spreads his huge wings and flies perplexedly around the room. Choosing her moment, Sea Girl grasps the key and escapes from the palace.

She makes for the forest and opens the locked-in waters of the lake with the golden key, and the torrent pours down the mountain side, quenching the parched meadows and bringing refreshment to the dry throats of the village.

1. You may use the story for a shadow theatre project or for mime.

2. For the shadow theatre you will need a screen made from a sheet and a strong light.

You will also need to make a cardboard cut-out for each character in the story.

3. There are many places in the story where music would be helpful. Each character, for example, could be introduced by his own tune.

Make a list of the music you need and share the job of composing it. Use notes D, E, G, A and B.

4. Choose a narrator, rehearse the music well, and you will be ready to produce the play.

5. Write a story of your own, suitable for a shadow theatre. Compose your own musical score.

BELL RINGING

This project is about the old English tradition of bell ringing. You need 8 people and 8 chime bars of the following pitches:

Form a circle in order of pitch.

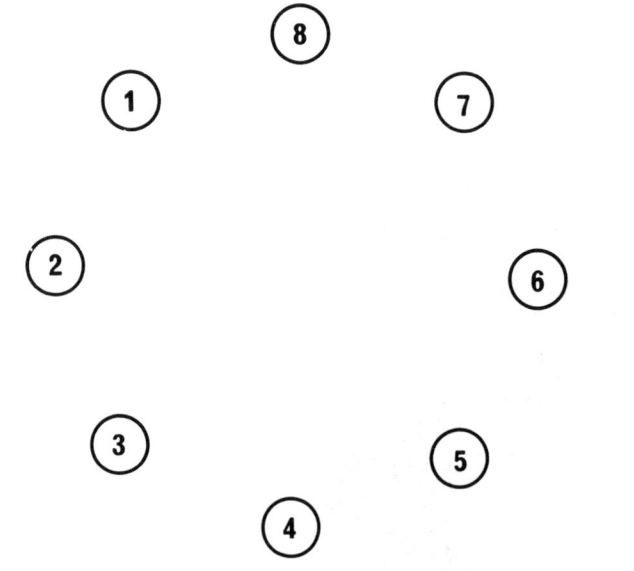

First practise ringing 'rounds'. Begin with 8 and move around the circle, 7, 6, 5, 4, 3, 2, 1, 8, 7, 6 and so on, until you can ring evenly. Now try speeding up. This needs special care and concentration.

You may also try 'change' ringing. This means changing the order of bells each time. Bell ringers often work from a chart like this:

```
8 7 6 5 4 3 2 1
7 8 6 5 4 3 2 1
7 6 8 5 4 3 2 1
7 6 5 8 4 3 2 1   and so on.
```

Notice how 8 moves back one place each time.

Make up changing patterns of your own and practise playing them.

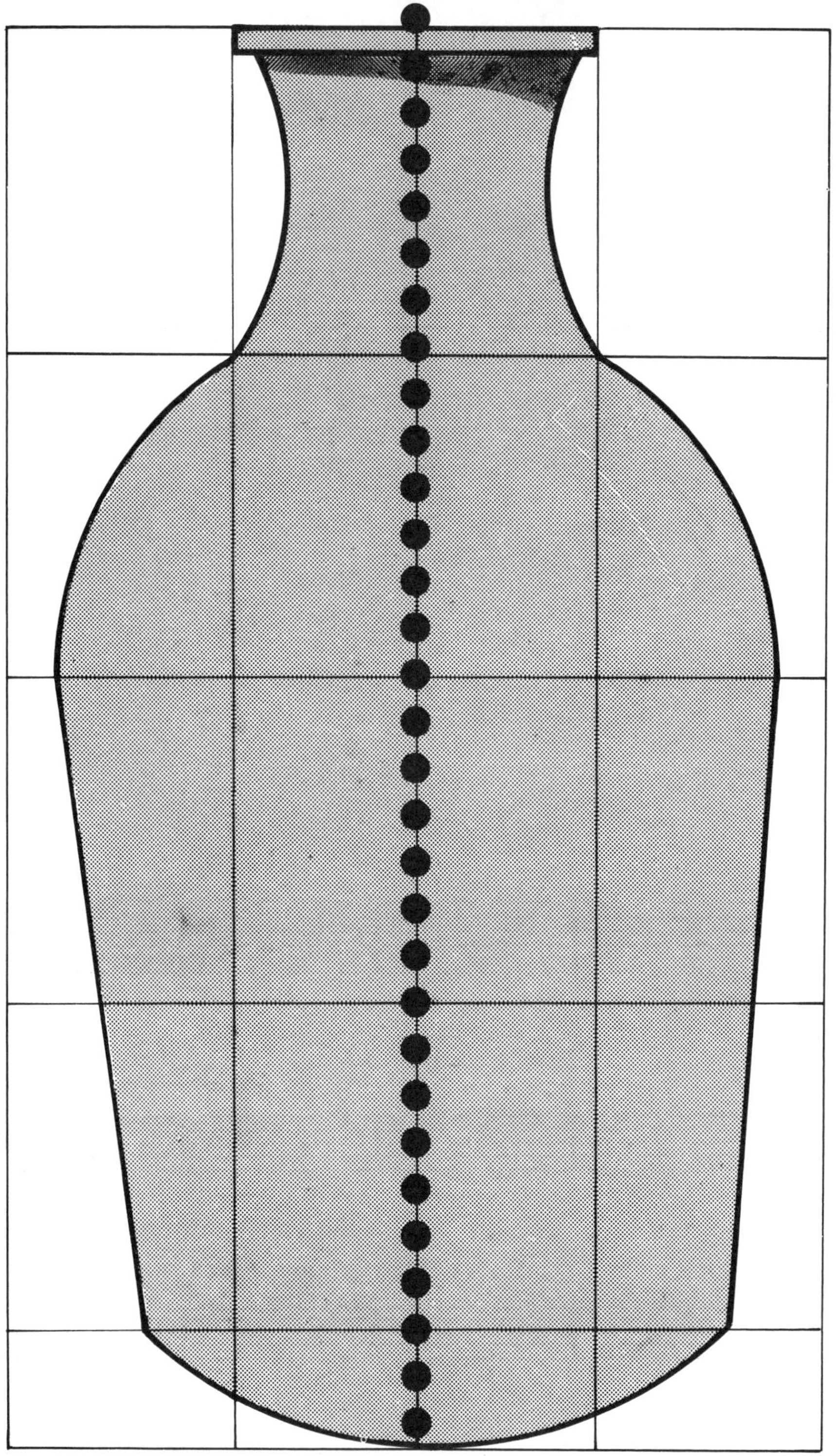

FORM
DISCOVERY

1. Most things in nature, like trees or flowers, grow in a balanced way.

   We can draw a line down the middle and one side is like the mirror of the other. This sort of balance is called symmetry. A human being has symmetry.

   Draw a line down the middle, and both sides match, with one eye, one ear, one arm and one leg each.

2. Many of the objects which men build have symmetry:
   buildings
   furniture
   pottery, and so on.

   How many examples can you think of?

3. Music has the same sort of balance. There is always the feeling that one part is balancing the other, like the question and answer exercises earlier in the book.

COMPOSITION

Melodies are made up of 'phrases'. One phrase balances the other. Here is an example:

PHRASE ONE   PHRASE TWO

Notice how phrase two has the same rhythm as phrase one. The tune, however is like a reflection of phrase one.

phrase one moves in this shape
phrase two moves in this shape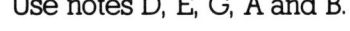

Make up phrases to balance the following tunes. Use an instrument to help you. Always end up on '**doh**'. Use the rhythm of the first phrase if you wish. Try to make your idea a reflection of the tune.
Use notes D, E, G, A and B.

Printed by Watkiss Studios Ltd., Biggleswade, Beds. 6/89